OF

WHITE TRASH

First published in 2005 by
New Holland Publishers (UK) Ltd
London • Cape Town • Sydney • Auckland
www.newhollandpublishers.com

Garfield House
86–88 Edgware Road
London W2 2EA
United Kingdom

14 Aquatic Drive
Frenchs Forest
NSW 2086
Australia

80 McKenzie Street
Cape Town 8001
South Africa

218 Lake Road
Northcote, Auckland
New Zealand

2 4 6 8 10 9 7 5 3 1

Publishing Manager: Jo Hemmings
Project Editor: Gareth Jones
Copy Editor: Sarah Larter
Designer: Alan Marshall
Production: Joan Woodroffe

Reproduction by Modern Age Repro House Ltd, Hong Kong
Printed and bound by Craft Print International Pte Ltd, Singapore

ISBN 1 84330 900 9

A TO Z

OF
WHITE TRASH

DARREN PIKE AND LEE QUICK
Photography by JAMIE SAME

NEW HOLLAND

CONTENTS

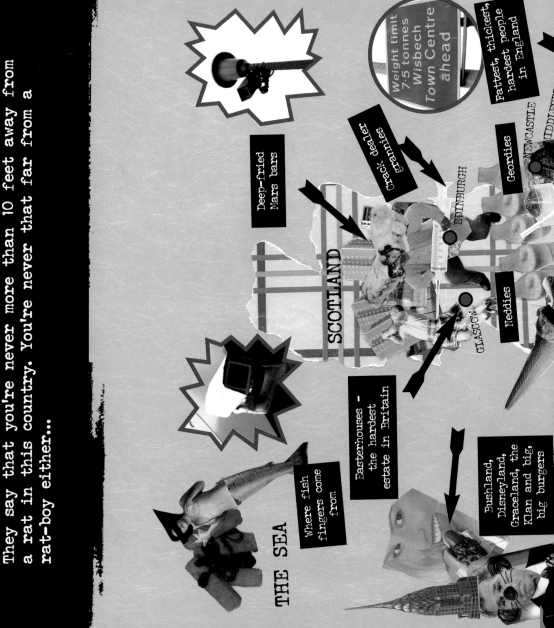

WHITE TRASH BRITAIN

They say that you're never more than 10 feet away from a rat in this country. You're never that far from a rat-boy either...

Weight limit
7·5 tonnes
Wisbech
Town Centre
ahead

Fattest, thickest, people
in England

Crack dealer
grannies

Deep-fried
Mars bars

EDINBURGH

Geordies

NEWCASTLE

SCOTLAND

Neddies

GLASGOW

Easterhouses -
the hardest
estate in Britain

Bushland,
Disneyland,
Graceland, the
Klan and big,
big burgers

Where fish
fingers come
from.

THE SEA

A is for...

A & E/Accident & Emergency: Where every half-decent Friday or Saturday night should end after binge-drinking, Ecstasy, GHB or smack-related overdoses – or a lethal combination of the afore-mentioned. Pick a fight with a nurse and sue later. *See* Compo.

Adidas: On everything. Even written in flowers on your coffin lid.

Aftershock: A drink available in red, blue and green. Useful when even a Stella with a Malibu chaser fails to bring your pills on.

A&E: It's midnight, friday, and you've just won compensation bingo!

Airports: Populated by pensioners in leisure gear, smoking like laboratory beagles, and hen parties spraying so much Duty Free tester that the air constitutes one part carbon monoxide to two parts Glow by J-Lo.

Air-rage: An EasyJet plane dive-bombs Luton when pensioners riot because they can't light a fag on take-off. *See also* Hen Parties.

Alcopops: Designed to mask the taste of moonshine-strength alcohol with diabetes-inducing levels of sugar. More dangerous than E. *See also* Ecstasy.

Aldi: Random German canned goods you've never heard of at flood-damaged prices. Useful when Iceland's just too posh. *See also* Iceland.

All-Inclusive Holidays: Two weeks all-in in the Dominican Republic with as much banana punch as you can drink from a bucket – and you never have to meet the natives. You realize why it was so cheap when the hurricane hits and the complex ends up in Haiti courtesy of a mudslide. You live to tell the tale on ITV's *Holidays from Hell* or *Trisha*.

Alloy Wheels: Stolen-to-order for a 20-year-old Ford Cortina that has been made to look like a high-performance car... But it doesn't. It looks like a 20-year-old Ford Cortina with alloys on.

All-You-Can-Eat Restaurants: The new post-pub curry in Chinese, pasta and pizza flavours. Fortunately you're too bollocksed on Diamond White to notice you're eating something put down on *Pet Rescue*. *See also* Diamond White.

Ambulance Chasers: No-win, no-fee lawyers who only ever advertise on daytime TV and specialize in spurious compensation claims. A cracked paving stone appears outside Iceland and the skies blacken as the entire population of the estate hurls itself at it. *See also* Compo.

American Pit Bull: A dangerous member of the family, a bit like Nanna, but with its own teeth. *See also* Dangerous Dogs.

Amusement Arcades: Paedophiles and penny-push machines. Rat-boys mugging grannies for their bingo winnings.

Ankles: To be shown in all weathers peeking out of sock-less trainers and three-quarter-length trackie bottoms. Underplay thick ankles with clever use of a £19.99 nine-carat gold LOVE anklet from Elizabeth Duke at Argos.

Alloys: When your wheels cost more than your motor.

Ann Summers Sex Parties: Hen parties pissing themselves about fluorescent condoms and strawberry-flavoured men's kegs. If they'd invented a vibrator that also mowed the lawn, Mum would have had Dad bumped off years ago.

£4.50 HOT BUFFET EAT AS MUCH AS YOU LIKE

Anti-Asylum Seeker Campaigns: After a couple of weeks living in Dover, Lee-on-Solent, or Stoke, having firebombs lobbed at you by SS pensioners, a life in Tehran seems somehow appealing. *See also* Racism, Xenophobia and Lee-on-Solent.

Anti-Paedophile Campaigns: A modern-day witch-hunt that has captured the imagination of the nation. A fun way of getting rid of anyone you don't like the look of. Special mention needs to be made of the Gwent locals who forced a doctor out of her home because she was a paediatrician. And who can forget Portsmouth's Paulsgrove Estate, where residents rioted, overturned cars, attacked council offices and generally ran amok, smashing the place up?

Anti-paedophile campaigns: Torch the neighbours!

Anti-Social Behaviour Order (ASBO): Status symbol and fast-track way to move house or appear on ITV's *Neighbours from Hell*.

Anti-Traveller Campaigns: The Firle Bonfire Society in Sussex wheeled a caravan with the registration 'P1KEY' and a mannequin dressed as a traveller on to the village green.. then set it on fire for a laugh.

Arses: Get them out after chucking-out time to pull a shag or goad the police. Once the distinguishing feature of white van man, now, thanks to G-strings and hipsters, birds' backsides are also on display. Tattoo your kids' names across your arse, so strangers know them, even when you've forgotten them.

Arson: Fun with matches.

· *Art* ·

A

Arsehole Mouth: Pursed, tight little round mouth found in conjunction with a rock-solid, wet-look, gelled top-knot. A close relative of lockjaw.

Arson: Can't sell it? Torch it. Claim it. Sorted!

Art: (1) Found in Clinton Cards in the precinct. (2) Celebrity tattoos like a Posh, Becks, Robbie or even Britney's Fairy – not to be confused with a Brittany Ferry. *See also* Boozecruise, Tattoos.

Artex: The Egyptians left cuneiform, the Greeks left marble. You leave artex.

Aunty: A non-related friend of Mum, or Dad's new girlfriend.

Australia: Birmingham overspill at the arse-end of the Earth. Paradise with wallabies and melanoma.

Ayia Napa: It's like Newcastle, only hot. Gang-raping squaddies, more holiday reps than you can shake a packet of 10 fags at, battle of the bars in Bar Square and bizarre moped deaths.

Arses: A small arse means big pants; a big arse means a G-string up your batty crack.

Artex: Wallpaper braille for when you're so pissed you can't find your way out of the pub.

11

B is for...

Baby: Also known as 'Baybee'. Remove the definite article (the) and you have a child that requires no first name or any title at all. For example: 'Ah, look at Baybee'; 'Mum/Mam, Baybee's swallowed one of your Es!'; 'Go on, Orlando/Chernice/Chardonnay/Keanu, say, "Hello" to Baybee'. (2) A useful decoy for store detectives while you're shoplifting at Lakeside. (3) A device for transporting Class-A drugs while you're visiting your boyfriend who's doing time in prison for twocking. *See also* TWOC/Twocking.

Back Of A Lorry: It's not stealing, it's economizing.

Bad: It's good.

Badger Baiting: Popular entertainment for those in the country-side with no access to burger bars, Argos or tanning salons. Toss the corpses onto the motorway as road-kill afterwards.

Balti: Dish served by Asian restaurateurs having the last laugh at thick Brummies who'd otherwise be eating pork scratchings, faggots and peas. The best thing to come out of Birmingham since the M6.

Bangers And Beans: Essential fart fuel in a tin. Little dogs' cocks floating in bean juice. When Mum gets pissed she lights her farts for a party trick and her shellsuit goes up like a torch.

Barratt Estates: Piss elegant pissy houses for pissy people.

Baseball Caps: As worn by Chavs, Charvers, mams with prams, Nanna and her pit bull Jamelia, these are worn day

'Dar-ren! Where's Baybee..?!?'

and night and never taken off. To be worn under a hooded top for that ultimate 'Ninja Turtle' rat-boy look. We await news of the first surgical fitting of a prosthetic baseball cap. *See also* Hoodies.

Bass (Sub Woofer): Giant in-car speakers that produce bass notes so low and loud that they damage hearing and cause blindness, impotence and loss of bowel control. And that's just the people in adjacent postal districts.

Bazza: A rat-boy's older brother. He's got a perm so tight you could bounce a coin off it. He spends his weekends at car boot sales and enjoys battle re-enactments.

BBQ: Cremated meat, marinated in Dad's lager and seasoned with fag ash... Sweet.

Young, old, fat, thin... If it breathes, cap it.

Beckham mohawk:
'...A-ga-doo-doo-dooo...!'

Beauty Therapy Course: Career girl! They'll teach you how to wear a white coat so shoppers think you're an atomic scientist, but you'll just end up flogging prawn sandwiches over the counter at Boots.

Beckham Mohawk: Also known as the Hoxton fin or mullet; a highlighted ridge on the top of the head with a lamb's tail at the back. Sported by the more fashionable and gayer end of the rat-boy spectrum, who think it makes them look like David Beckham. But it doesn't, they just look like those blokes who sang *Agadoo*.

Beer Belly: Blubber cascading from beneath a cropped top. *See also* Boob Tubes, Crop Tops.

Bella Brusco: Best drunk at the approximate temperature of a bus shelter.

Belly-Button Piercing: (1) A constant reminder to Mum that when they cut your umbilical cord she should have kept the giblets and flushed you down the sluice. (2) A device that sets off the alarm when you're trying to shoplift a frozen chicken from Iceland. *See also* Piercings.

BBQ: Twelve big tins of Tennents Extra followed by an uncooked sausage. You get shit-faced and chuck a can of diesel on the fire so that the whole estate can share in the fesitivities.

Beach Wedding: Your white meringue blowing in the tropical breeze and your whole family yakking up with the Norwalk virus while dressed in full morning dress. All of which is lovingly captured on video and set to music. But you get the weather...

Beauty Therapy: Putting your slap on has never sounded so scientific – botox, nail-bars, liposuction, plucked eyebrows and tanning sprays. *See also* Plastering.

Body-piercing, or proof
that even stretch
denim has its limits?

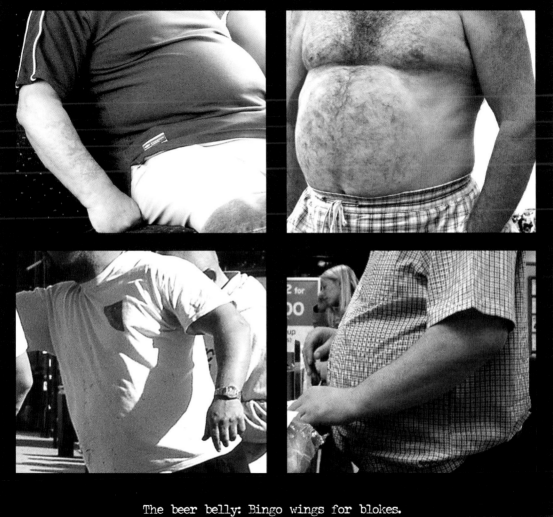

The beer belly: Bingo wings for blokes.

Bingo: (1) Venue with spiral carpeting the size of a Baltic state that's full of hen parties and grannies competing for shit prizes, which revolve behind glass. (2) The only reason to buy a tabloid apart from the footie results and/or a guide to starting an anti-paedophile campaign.

Bingo Wings: Under-arm cellulite deposits. 'Bingo!' yells Aunty Sandra, arms aloft, flapping her waddles in a haze of fag smoke. Best displayed in lemon sleeveless tops.

Benidorm: Croydon-on-Sea...

Ben Sherman Shirts: Always worn untucked.

Benson and Hedges: Also known as B&H or Bensons, as in 'Sandra, where's my Bensons?' *See also* Fags.

Berghaus Coat: Or is it a burger bar overall and you're flipping them?

Billericay: The town that put Essex-chic on the map. It's celebrated for Barratt homes, ankle chains, mini skirts and tans in sub-zero temperatures. Populated by cockney wankers in designer gear driving about in open soft-tops, whatever the weather.

Binge Drinking: Washes down your breakfast.

BINGO EVERY NIGHT EXCEPT TUES & THURS

Birdie Song, The: Shit-faced pensioners pissing themselves while doing chicken movements.

Birds of a Feather: Flock together? The fat bird from *Being April*, the other one with the lockjaw, and Lesley Joseph, sulk while playing themselves so Essex can laugh at itself. O, flock off!

Birthday Parties: 14-year-olds get pissed and joyride a Vauxhall Nova into a bus shelter full of pensioners.

Bling is king! Solid 9ct shite — standard!

Blackpool: White Trash mecca. Like the sea, the tourists are rough and full of chemicals. Populated with rat-boys getting their arses out along the Golden Mile, girl gangs getting their tits out on the Pepsi Max and pensioners getting their tits out on big coaches.

Bling: African-American hip-hop-inspired term for postmodern nouveau-riche vulgarian jewellery that's now used for anything that sparkles, for example: thick gold necklaces, sovereign rings, diamanté teeth, Nanna's gold mac. Confirmation that all that glitters is not gold. *See also* Goldette.

Body kits: Changing Rooms for cars.

Blinglish: The language of bling. Unfortunately, you're white, not black, but why let that stop you from speaking in Jamaican patois? Example: 'Me and me hench is coching and I'm like, "Catch dis buff bitch!" And me hench is like, "She's a mampi, innit!" Razklatt. Standard!' – Darren, aged 15 from Wisbech. *See also* Wiggerspeak.

Blokes bogs: Slash, spit,
don't wash, and go.

Blokes' Bogs: Place to slash on used chewing gum and those pineapple-cube things in the urinals, while you're waiting to score some Es.

BOBFOC: 'Body Off *Baywatch*, Face Off *Crimewatch*'. Ropey old birds with hair braids doing step-aerobics and getting off with geezers half their age. Raddled turkey neck, but nice calf muscles. *See also* Face That Would Stop A Train, Tanning Salons.

Body Kit: Bits of plastic from Halfords that get stuck on a Vauxhall Nova. For that Formula One look, as you joyride into a bus shelter full of pensioners.

Body-Popping Challenges: At a bus-stop in your old skool white Lacoste shell suit – but you don't fight, you *dance*! Only you're in Addington.

3% beer squash: Drink loads and never get pissed... Well 'ard!

Boob Tubes: Ill-fitting, but great for getting your tits out in a hurry. Although if they were never in how can you get them out? *See also* Beer Belly, Crop Tops.

Bookies: Great place for Nanna to deal her mazzies to the junkies and place a bet on the dogs. *See also* Mazzie.

Books: For poofs and toffs. Unless it's the Argos catalogue.

Boozecruise: Cross-Channel excursions on a ferry to buy industrial quantities of fags and booze. Mark them up and flog them on at a car boot sale. *See also* Car Boot Sales.

Bottle: (1) Also known as 'bockle' by the verbally dyslexic and thick. (2) A vessel to be pissed into and lobbed at others in pedestrianized shopping streets at chucking-out time. (3) Cockney wankers' bollocks, as in, "Ee's lost 'is fackin' bottle!" – *lit.* 'He is rather afraid.'

Boyracer: Chavs attempt to impress their girlfriends by saying how many cars they've 'totalled' and by never driving at anything less than twice the speed limit.

Brand Names: The bigger the better when purchasing clothes, but never when it comes to buying stuff from the supermarkets. Big it up for own-brand cola!

Brazil: (1) A full-shave downstairs. (2) A favoured destination after a prison break-out. In either case, an area of disappearing jungle.

Bread: Stuff found on either side of a burger.

Breakfast: Have your first fag of the day with a packet of Quavers!

Bricks: (1) Implements for welcoming asylum seekers, suspected paedophiles, or your new neighbours to the estate. (2) A support for your car after those little bastards fleeced your alloys.

Brown Babies: 'I wanna brahn baby, Wayne, like the other mums on the estate.' As popularized by Waynetta Slob.

Brown Sauce: With everything. Not to be confused with what makes brown babies.

Want to taste Daddy's Sauce?

Bruises: Preferably purple and going yellow-green. A great way of showing that you've had a shag, had a fight or recently injected a vein with smack.

Buckie: Buckfast wine – lovingly made by Devonshire Monks and guzzled by neds in Scotland.

Budget Airline: Conveyance that carries hen parties on binge-drinking trips abroad.

Budgies: Horrible little creatures that shit all over the place and can be taught words like 'wanker' and 'cock off'. Just like the kids.

Builders' Arses: Like the first cuckoos of spring, so it is with the first builder's arse of the season. By summer, they're in full song, farting loudly from the scaffolding.

Nothing beats crisps and a cig for a nutritious brekkie.

Bull Terrier: Staffordshire, English or Mastiff. *See also* Dangerous Dogs.

Bumps: When your big sister gives you the bumps on your birthday, she means a blast on her charlie and ketamine ('CK') chasers.

Burger Bar: Where you go when you're bunking off school and someone's already shat in the bus shelter. The bogs are a good place to freebase your smack. It's also the venue of choice for Chardonnay's birthday party or the little get-together you have after Grandad's cremation.

Bruises: Yellow, green, purple... Get well soon.

Builder's cleavage: Cheeky!

Burgers: Ear 'oles, eye 'oles and arse'oles. 'Do you want fries with that?'

C is for...

Caff: Fast-food outlets from the Neolithic period, where the staff wear nylon tabards and smoke fags behind the counter. The red sauce bottles look like plastic tomatoes.

Capo di Monte: Luxury at affordable prices: ladies in big dresses, children in bonnets, tramps on park benches and a series of dangerous dog breeds all immortalized in porcelain. Stick them on top of the flat screen.

Capo di Monte:
Very affordable.

Caravan: Kept in front of the house on bricks, it's where Nanna does her drug dealing. Heaven is a nice static caravan with a chip pan and a chemical toilet.

Car Boot Sales: Weekends spent walking through a mud bath and buying knock-off fags out of the back of a Mazda. You can't escape the

The Caff: Bad food, milky tea, greasy walls – it's like a home from home.

smell of donuts and dead grannies.

Career: Sweeping up bits of hair waiting to get pregnant. *See also* CSA (Child Support Agency).

Careworker: If you have one of these you're one up from a tagging device and one step short of watching SKY Sports all day in a young offenders' unit.

Cash-In-Hand: What the Benefits don't know, don't hurt 'em.

21

Casinos: Bingo for geezers.

Catalogues: The only book in the house apart from *Take a Break* and the instructions for the mobile. Where you can buy clothes at 20 pence a week for about 400 years. You get down behind the settee when the catalogue woman comes knocking at your door on a Friday.

Catalogue shops: Queuing at a counter just like when you're waiting for Job Seekers' Allowance, only this is for plastic garden furniture.

CCTV: A good reason to wear Nanna's tights over your head, but make sure you diddle them under a tap first.

CD Compilations: Titles include the *Now That's What I Call The Best Ever Christmas Adverts You've Heard Medley Number 3,565,789* album, or anything by Jane McDonald.

Celebrity Workout Videos: Step aerobics in front of the telly. Eat a bag of chips in a sweatband afterwards.

Central Heating: On full blast even when the flagstones are cracking outside in June. A prime cause of corned-beef legs. *See also* Corned-Beef Legs.

Chains: Gold-like or goldette, thick and spine-disfiguringly heavy. Hanging outside your zip-up leisure gear like the homeboys in da hood. Well, that's how your careworker likes to wear hers anyhow. *See also* Bling, Goldette.

Catalogue stores: Where you learn to read Part I

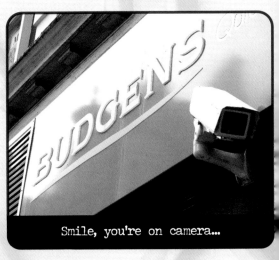

Smile, you're on camera...

Channel 5: Films, footie and fucking.

Chardonnay: (1) Character from ITV's *Footballers' Wives*. (2) Posh wine. Nice body but really cheap and tarty.

Charlotte Church: Christenings and funerals wouldn't be the same without *Pie Jesu*.

Chart: Music.

Chav: Originally from Chatham; now, like dog-shit, Chavs are found everywhere, especially in Guildford.

Charvers: The female of the species is more deadly than the male.

Chelsea Smile: A cheek-splitting scar that's been earned during a brawl at closing time, or at the on-the-turn counter in the supermarket for the last of the bread.

Goldette overload: Fat slag chic.

The larger the chain, the lower the life form.

Chewing gum: Also known as chuddy, it's stuffed in kids' mouths to stop the crying just after they've had their ears pierced. Eaten noisily 24/7, always with the mouth open. It is never, ever removed from the mouth, not even when eating chips or shagging.

Chewy: *See* Love-bite.

Chicken Nuggets: Reconstituted chicken product full of beak, claws and bol-locks. The ideal snack for busy mams with prams who haven't got time for a full super-size. Dip in BBQ-flavour creosote sauce to taste. Eat on the bottom deck of a bus.

Child Smoker: Prodigy.

Chins: Double, treble, or last nights' tea found in.

Chip Butty: Carbohydrate and fat and more carbohydrate and fat. It's top.

Chip Pan: Traditional implement for torching the house, garden and half the street. Now in decline thanks to the advent of microwave chips. Posh people don't have chip pans, they eat muesli instead.

Chippendale Video: Aunty Trish hits freeze-frame on the remote and flicks herself off over a bloke's bits.

Chips: Food for life.

Chip Shop: Place to arse about outside of that's one up from the bus shelter.

Chips, Oven: Progress.

Chips, Microwave: Pure rocket science.

Chip Wallpaper: Like you've flicked chip bits all over the walls and they've stuck.

Chippy: (1) The chip shop. (2) A geezer called Wayne who planes door frames and pisses in your sink.

Chucking out time: Ding, ding! Round One! Grab a bockle and pick a window.

Church: (1) Charlotte. (2) A place to nick lead. (3) A place to have a big fuck-off wedding that costs the earth. The bride throws her bouquet at her bridesmaids, only to realise that she tossed them her fags instead. The groom wonders what he saw in someone 15 times his own body-mass. (4) The place to do Baybee's christening when the DNA test you took on *Trisha* reveals that it was yours after all.

Cider: Rural rat-boy juice. Homebrew. Next Stop A&E.

Cigarettes: The perfect accompaniment to chips and shagging, with extra points if all three are executed simultaneously. Bensons, Craven As, Embassy Number 5, Embassy Regal, JPS, Lambert & Butler, Super Kings, Mayfair, Rothmans or anything bought by the freight-load from a boozecruise. *See also* Boozecruise.

Chips: Health food...
Potatoes are healthy, innit?

chav /tʃæv/ *noun* (*BrE, slang, C20th*): Vulgar person, of poor intellect; individual member of social underclass, primarily characterized by an utter lack of taste. [*Deriv.* uncertain, possibly from *Chatham, Kent*]

Cigarettes: The world is your ashtray.

A day at the seaside: Minding the kids while your missus gets the chips in.

Clairvoyants: Phone the 1-2-1 Psychic Hotline on the back of *Take a Break* to find out from Grandad where he left the spanner for the stop-cock before he died.

Classical Music: For poofs, unless it's the stuff played at the World Cup or anything by Opera Babes or Enya.

Club 18–30: Organised sex games with squirty cream and vegetables shaped like a bloke's cock. You're guaranteed alcohol poisoning and sunstroke while you're there but the only thing you'll bring back home since they abolished Duty Free is the clap. *See* Club Rep.

Club Comedians: A bubble perm you could go trick-or-treating in and racist jokes that would make Ann Winterton MP blush. Great family entertainment.

Club Rep: Top job ever. You don't need languages, just to be able to organize drinking games and get your cock or tits out. You go back to Wisbech at the end of the season.

Coach: Pensioner transport for day-trips to Pwllheli, Rhyl or Blackpool, or a geezer conveyance to another town so you can kick the shit out of rival footie gangs. Usually promises to involve racist chants, moonies out of the back window and robbing the driver's collection. But that's today's pensioners for you.

Coastal Towns: For example, Dover, Great Yarmouth, Hull, Lee-on-Solent and Skegness. Modern-day seaside attractions include injecting heroin, attacking asylum seekers and girl gangs running down the prom with their tits out. You never wear a coat in these places, whatever the weather.

Cocaine: Also known as charlie or coke. You get yours cheap from Liz who minds l'il Keanu at daycare.

Cockney Birds: As exemplified by *EastEnders'* Kat Slater, or Daniella...

Cockney Wankers: Cheeky chappy market traders who say words like 'gowz' meaning 'girls' and 'sustif-cat' for 'certificate'.

Coco-Pops: Never eaten for breakfast – that's time for Quavers.

Coke and Fags: Having a bit of coke with your fags – the legal version.

Collectibles: If it's from a shit-shop or a bit of tat bought out the back of a car in a boot sale, chances are it's found shelf-space in your home. You've collected 12 ornamental thimbles at £19.99 each plus P&P from a Sunday colour supplement, and they threw in a wall-mounted mahogany-effect rack. You've got an alabaster sculpture of dolphins leaping out of the sea on top of the flat screen, and a limited-edition debutante collection of china ladies with their dresses blowing in the wind. There's a series of Care Bear and Pokémon miniature figurines in poly-resin in the bay window. Why is it that ornamental plate collections always commemorate the Battle of Britain?

Combats: Camouflage trousers worn by Urban Chavs, copied off *East 17* who in turn nicked it off Gay Skinheads. Well 'ard.

Community Service: Two weeks cleaning windows at the day centre for the disabled, or wiping pensioners' arses while wearing a tagging device.

Compo: The compensation culture that allows you to sue every-one, even the bloke whose flat-screen TV you robbed because it can't get any of the Sky channels.

Britain's finest hour.

'I've got the real thing in my handbag, if you fancy it, Trace.'

Conservatories: Plastic lean-tos that get so hot in summer they melt your goldette necklace. Useful for when you're dealing and it gets too busy for the caravan. At least your charlie stays dry in here.

Conspicuous Consumption: It's not what you wear, it's how much it cost and how many people you tell.

Conversation: 'OK right, she's going like this to me, right? Like all this, you know? And I'm like, so totally, whatever. You know? And she goes "O yeah?" like that to me. And I'm like, "Yeah, what about it?" She's like "Yeah? Yeah?... O, yeah?" and all that, you know? So I goes, right, "Yeah right!" And then she's just like, "Whatever!"'. Transcript of a mobile phone conversation overheard on the 159 bus to Streatham.

Council house facelift: Wet look gel as urban armour.

Corned-Beef Legs: Unattractive condition caused by central heating, sitting too close to a two-bar electric fire or when you've no more veins to inject in the rest of your body.

Costa Del Sol/Costa Blanca: Paradise for those who can't be bothered to travel to Australia or whose arses are too big for a standard long-haul economy seat.

Council: The people who told you to bury Grandad when he started to smell.

Council Flat: Bought, posh fuckers. *See also* Giro Drop.

Council-House Facelift: Take a scrunchie, pull back your hair so it looks like you've been caught in a G-force, add a gelled fringe, hoopies and a fag... You're looking good.

Courtship: As in 'Tits first, I'm no slag!' You're thinking 'Is this the streak of piss I'd like my kids to spend every other weekend with?'

Cowboys: Flags of St George hanging off ladders on white vans meets country-and-western rustling. They'll artex your ceilings and appear on ITV's *Builders from Hell*, pissing in your sink or sniffing the knickers in your drawers. Your supporting walls would be safer put in contact with a bulldozer than one of these. Add arses hanging out of trackies and Radio 1, and you're in Hell.

Crazy pebbledashing...

Crazy Paving: Vandalism in the form of multi-coloured slabbing. Driveways for the taste-impaired.

Credit Cards: Great for chopping your charlie, breaking and entering, defrauding, getting into shit-loads of debt and eventually appearing in court.

Crew: Also known as krew, gang, posse or squad. Membership consists of hooded rat-boys giving the finger at bus stops.

Crimewatch: 'Mum, It's Darren with Nanna's tights on his head!'

Criminal Record: (1) GBH, armed robbery, dealing or benefit fraud. (2) *I Will Survive*, *Everything I Do (I Do It For You)* and Celine's theme from *Titanic*.

Crisps: Sometimes pronounced 'crips', these are the healthy option when the chippy's shut, and also the ideal convenience food for when Mum's not to be disturbed in her bedroom with 'Uncle' Dave.

Crop Tops: Best worn if you're a 15-stone tanorexic. Popular in Wisbech. *See also* Beer Belly, Boob Tubes, Tanning Salons.

Croydon Pineapple: Hair spurting out of a top-knot scrunchie like a gelled Vesuvius. *See also* Croydon Smile.

Croydon Smile: Facial seizure inflicted by scrunchies. Essential for navigating concrete spiral staircases and pedestrianized shopping streets with a pram in, well, Croydon.

Cruises: The Dover to Calais fag-run, only you never get off. Jane McDonald serenades pensioners who are throwing up with food poisoning. And everyone's in a shell suit.

Cruising: Fleets of souped-up Novas racing the streets of Southend.

CSA (Child Support Agency): Income once you've hung up the hair-sweeping brush for the last time.

Cuppa: The only answer when you're spitting feathers.

Curfew: A device used by the police for keeping thieving rat-boys indoors, other than smack on delivery and *Trisha*.

Curry sauce: goes with everything. Even the colour of your teeth.

The Croydon Pineapple: For that soft, glaring look when you want summfink off him...

D is for...

Dad: Identified by DNA then fleeced by the CSA.

Dado Rails: Every living room needs them, preferably painted in dusky rose or peach with spray-on gold stencilling.

Dangerous Dogs: It's hard, you're hard, preferred breeds include American Pit Bulls, Rottweilers (always pronounced 'rot-wheel-ers') and wire-haired mongrels with names like Jamelia, Shelley or Cunt. For rural White Trash, a pet dog that'll take a badger on is a bonus. *See also* Girl Gangs.

Daniella: As in 'having a Daniella'. The point when you've consumed so much charlie that your nose disintegrates.

Darts: The sport where you can smoke, fart, swear and drink your entire family's body weight in lager.

Day-glo Lipstick: Tit-pink lippy sported by glamour models to draw attention away from their tits. *See also* Glamour Modelling.

Daytime TV: Make some noise for *Trisha*, *Glamorous Granny Makeovers* and Fern Britten!

Dealer: Bloke you get your gear off when Nanna's in Calais for the day.

Debts: What you owe your dealer.

Deck: What your dealer does to you when you can't pay your debts.

Dentistry: An entire set of false teeth by the age of 17, with gold and diamanté the preferred option if you're flush. *See also* False Teeth.

Daytime TV: DNA results within the hour.

Designer Labels: It's not what you wear, but how expensive it was. Tel is sent down for his last joyriding offence in Versace, and Aunty Sandra's sporting a Nike shellsuit for her third wedding. Not to be worn if you fancy binge-drinking in Leicester, where all the main pubchains have banned designer gear like Burberry. Other proscribed labels include Aquascutum, Henri-Lloyd, Stone Island and Rockport (Rockies). However, George at ASDA is fine. *See also* Fake Designer Labels.

Diamond White: Apple fruit drink that's the alcoholic graduation from Sunny D.

Disco Buffet: Sausage rolls, cheese and pineapple on cocktail sticks, tinned pink salmon mashed with vinegar, tuna vol-au-vents, black forest gateaux and a big fuck-off trifle. They turn off the mobile disco when the buffet opens.

DNA Test: Here's Daddy! *See also Trisha.*

'D'ja nah 'ta mean?': Used to end a sentence when 'standard', 'innit' or 'cunt' won't do. *See also* Innit.

Doctors: Place you visit when you need a stress-related sicknote.

Dogging: Brummies ostensibly walking dogs on Cannock Chase, but getting up to mucky business in and out

Dangerous dogs...
And their pitbulls.

Designer labels:
Spell it big! Fashion
flash cards for the
teen illiterati.

BAK

Mock baronial stone cladding and alloy double glazing.

of each other's Vauxhall Novas instead. No dogs are involved in the actual sex acts... Well, not the canine variety anyway.

Dog Shit: It's everywhere. Still it's preferable to the junkie shit all over the estate.

Dog Track: Catford, Romford or any pedestrianized street populated with girl gangs after chucking-out time.

Domestic Violence: Also known as 'having a domestic'.It's terrace-rage violence played out in front of the kids and the flat-screen TV... Mum knocks Dad out sparko, then dumps him at A&E.

Doormen: Jobs for ex-squaddies, ex-coppers, ex-offenders and ex-husbands.

Double-Glazing: Ripping out the original features of your house to replace them with aluminium and plastic.

Drug-Dealing Grannies: Examples include the one from Edinburgh who dealt to the customers in the café where she worked and another from the Raploch Estate in Stirling who set up an anti-paedophile campaign at the same time as dealing heroin from her own home. She and her family were then evicted from the estate before they all were sentenced as a job lot to a long prison term. Class!

Drugs: Uppers, downers, buying, selling... And that's just your kid brother.

Dykes: (1) Rough-as-fuck lesbians who'll have your face off. (2) Things that drained the fens, leaving Wisbech with Fen Folk.

Dyslexic: That's your careworker calling you thick.

'Dad, stop it! You're hurting me!"

JB'S PLACE
No Burberry
No Trainers
No Baseball Caps
No Hoodies
No Tracksuits

Warning

Fire exit keep clear

Dealers and drugs: Deserted stairways and underpasses? Don't all dealers deliver in 4x4s these days?

SHARPS BOX
SYRINGE DISPOSAL POINT

DOGGERS
Wanna get laid tonight?

s not just the Geordies going out for a bottle of dog.

33

is for...

Earn £££££££££££££££££££££££££££££££££££££ Adverts: Sweatshop-style home working while watching SKY Sports.

Earrings: The earlier ears are pierced the better. Get Baybee done before you leave the hospital. We await news of the first foetus to have studs gunned into its ears using keyhole surgery. Favoured styles include silver and diamanté sleepers for boys and big goldette hoops for girls. *See also* Bling.

***Eastenders*:** Cockney wankers with no brains and cockney birds with no septums.

Easterhouses: The hardest place in Scotland. Everything is hard – not least the drugs.

Ecstasy: Popularly known as E, it's cheaper than a pint and less effective these days. It's a great way to settle your stomach before you crack into the Malibu and coke. Rennies for the post-rave generation.

Elephantine: Aunty Sandra's gammy legs; kids generally these days.

Elizabeth Duke: Top jewellery ever.

Earn at home: Busty, mature, willing to travel, and that's just the punters...

Earrings: Always a good place to yank-start a fight.

Elvis Tribute Artistes: When the King of Rock-and-Roll becomes a postman who's singing in pubs and wearing stick-on sideburns, in Streatham or Telford.

Emmerdale: *Hollyoaks* on a farm. Lesbianism beside the silage pit.

Essex: Eastern county populated by snooker players and footballers' wives, living in fuck-off big mansions with kidney-shaped pools and chiming gates.

Estates: Only council, never country or cars.

Estuary: (1) Cockney-esque dialect; (2) The River Thames basin. Seems okay on the surface but is still full of shit.

Estuary English: Features the 'glottal stop', where the letter T is not pronounced in the middle of words such as 'bottle' (pronounced 'bo'al') and the diphthong in words like 'brown' is made like 'braan'. Not to be confused with 'Mockney', which is for posh cunts like Jamie Oliver and that violin-playing Nigel... English Estuary is soon to become Standard English pronunciation. Standard!

Exhaust: Always loud.

Expensive: *See* Conspicuous Consumption.

Eyebrow Piercing: Face jewellery. It smarts something rotten when it snags on your hoodie. *See also* Piercings.

Eyebrows: Plucked to fuck and so high that it looks as if you've got a permanently startled expression.

Eyesore: No matter how much pancake slap you trowel on, you're still a right sight.

'Fancy an E with your Quavers?'

Elvis: Still the King...

F is for...

Face That Would Stop A Train: *See* BOBFOC.

Faded Tattoos: DIY body art. A biro and a needle and you're off. LOVE, HATE, MUM, SANDRA, TRISH...

Fags: (1) Homosexuals. (2) Tabs. They leave brown stains in your mouth. The tabs, too. *See also* Benson and Hedges, Cigarettes.

Fake: Everything – even your teeth.

Fake Designer Labels: Who can forget Galvin Klein underpants or Rolf Lauren Polo Shirts on sale in Chorley market? For the ladies, feminize that Kappa Slappa look with a fake Louis Vuitton clutch bag to hold your mobile phone and fags. Sure to kick faux-Burberry's ass next season. *See also* Designer Labels.

False Teeth: Also known as wallies. When Nanna smiles under the ultra-violet light at the bingo, the hen party's maimed by the flash burn. *See also* Dentistry.

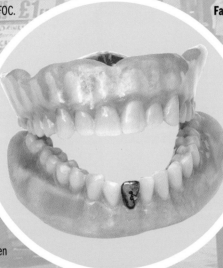

When you're kissing Nanna goodbye, mind your tongue doesn't pull her teeth out.

Family: 'Shut it, Mum, this is family!'

Family Bucket: That's one each. To be eaten in front of the flat-screen TV and accompanied by a big fuck-off bockle of Rola-Cola. It looks like the Mai Lai massacre took place on a battery farm.

Farting: Funny ice-breakers, unless it's a wet rasper that skids your undies. If you wear them, that is. Fingers crossed that you don't follow-through too.

Fast Food: Dead-end job – 'Do you want fries with that?', or slow death – 'Do you want a heart by-pass with that?'

Fat Fuckers: Once the rich were fat and the poor were thin. Now the rich are thin and the poor are fat, flush and fucking hard!

Fen Folk: *Lord of the Rings*-style inhabitants in places like Wisbech.

Faded tatts: How can they be faded? He hasn't had a wash in years.

Fake designer labels: Needs must, so you get a scaghead to nick it to order down the market.

Fence: (1) Device dividing you from your warring neighbours. (2) Person who sells the goods you stole to your warring neighbours.

Ferrets: Rural White Trash keep these to set on rabbits for fun. They're vicious, smelly buggers with yellow teeth. The ferrets, however, are quite pleasant.

Five-Finger Discount: One better than an BOGOF.

Fireworks: Launch a pet into space with a rocket up the cat-flap.

Fireworks: To be thrown at old ladies and blind people and also useful for seeing off those asylum seekers who moved to the estate. The reason why so many rat-boys have one eye or a botched skin graft.

Fast food: Chips on wheels.

F

Fish & Chips: Nah, it's dead posh now. Next up – deep-fat-fried pizza triangles and thick mushy peas inside a batter ball... With chips, obviously.

Fish Fingers: Darren's always had fish fingers... But that's because he can't keep his hands out of his pants.

Flabby Midriffs: If your midriff looks like that, what does your arse look like? *See also* Beer Belly.

Flat-Screen TV: With DVD, surround-sound and Dolby. A stand for Capo Di Monte and Royal memorabilia. *See also* Telly, Capo Di Monte, Royal Memorabilia.

Flob: I flob, he/she flobs, it flobs, you flob, we flob, they flob. We're all flobbing big greenies all over the great bus shelter of the world.

Wisbech flora.

These plants are for everyone's enjoyment Please do NOT touch them

Flowers: Buy them from the buckets outside the 24-hour garage, next to the bags of BBQ charcoal, or, alternatively rob a cemetery. When Darren gets all sentimental, he says it with flowers. Shelley says it back with a court injunction. Funerals are a deluge of carnations – sprays, baskets, heart-shaped wreaths and the Gates of Heaven ajar... It's like BBC's *Groundforce* has laid siege to the grave. Flowers are in big, fuck-off letters at the back of the hearse spelling out the names of the stiff in the back.

Flush: (1) Minted innit, loadsa money, job's a good 'un. (2) The rozzers turn up at Nanna's and she dumps her stash down the bog.

Totally Fucked Landscape
White Van Man (c.21st)

Fly-tipping: The only thing to happen in the country apart from badger baiting and incest. Drive to the arse end of nowhere and dump your rubbish. Makes a nice day out for the kids, too.

Football: The essence of life itself – 'The ref's a cunt'; 'That cunt was offside'; 'I've never seen such a bunch of cunts in all my life'; etc.

Football Shirts: As worn by fat old knackers with a pint in one hand, a fag in the other and a spider's web tattooed on their throats, shouting obscenities at passing buses. They do 'em for men too.

Footballers' Wives: Porsches, St. Tropez skin sprays, straightened hair, day-glo lipstick and coke snorted off false fingernails. Usually found in Essex or Cheshire.

Ford Orion: Body kit, go-faster stripes, flared wheel arches, vented bonnet, chrome tailpipe and under-car neon lighting... It's greased lightnin'! No it's not, it's stolen and it's over 20 years old.

Fred Perry: Old school leisure gear from back in the day, when Chavs' dads were called casuals.

Freezing Your Tits Off: You've never heard of a coat check. It's a Saturday night, it's –20°c with snow-drifts and Arctic gales and you're still out in a shirt throwing piss-filled bottles at each other or getting your tits/cock/arse out.

'Fruit' Juices: The kiddies just love that orange-flavoured Vitamin C drink. Sweet.

Funeral: You play *Pie Jesu*, *Wind Beneath My Wings*, *Grandad We Love You*, *Who Wants to Live for Ever*, garage and *My Heart Will Go On* as you go through the curtains. You also put a poem in the local paper. *See also* Poem.

Funfair: Flashing lights and paedophiles. Give the bloke on the dodgems a blow job and you and your mates'll get free rides all night...

Fur Coat: In tabby, tortoiseshell, ginger-tom or rat. To be worn down the precinct. With slippers.

Lee Quick's piss stains are luminous, but this has nothing to do with drinking Sunny D.

Football is life... From the cradle to the grave: for hatchings, matchings and dispatchings.

is for...

Gadgie: Old feller.

Game: (1) On the. (2) She's a game old bird. *See also* BOBFOC.

Garage: (1) Music played at Baybee's christening or Grandad's funeral. (2) An all-night service station where you can buy tabs and flowers from buckets.

Garden: Where Bazza tinkers about under a brick-supported car and Nanna does her dealing. Put down ornamental flagstones if you're flush.

Gary, Up the: What glamour models say they'll never do – unless it's for an extra 50 notes and their bus fare home. *See also* Glamour Modelling.

'In an English country garden...'

Gay Hotels: As found in Brighton, Bournemouth or Blackpool. 'Mein host' is called Frank or Barry and has a face like a slapped arse. He sprays industrial air-freshener in quantities that invoke memories of Bhopal, but the place still smells of sperm and chips. *See also* Piss Elegant.

Gay Trash: Stocky, short-necked couples sporting facial hair – and that's only the women. Male fashion-victims with Beckham mohawks, crop tops and flabby Celtic arm tattoos. Nice handbags though. *See also* Beckham Mohawk.

GBH/GHB: One slug and it's a near-death experience.

Dangerous dogs: 'Fuck off, cunt!'

Geezers: Big streaks of piss found mainly in Iceland. Or Lidl.

Gelled Fringe: A carefully groomed fringe that's gelled and highlighted. Known in South London as the Vauxhall Visa. *See also* Council-House Facelift, Offensive Hairstyles, Shit For Hair.

Geordies: The men are men and the women are men too, except they wear less, fuck dirtier and fight harder.

George at ASDA: High-quality fashion at affordable prices. Located at the bottom aisle next to the chicken rotisserie.

Ginsters Sausage Rolls: Traditional country-kitchen cooking straight out of the newsagents' microwave next to the Readers' Wives' kebabs.

Girl Gangs: Girls who say words like 'cunt' and generally don't give a fuck. Not the same as dangerous dogs, but should still be muzzled or put down. *See also* Dangerous Dogs.

Giro Drop: A second residence for that beneficiary of state benefits who never existed, or Dad's dog who died of mange 20 years ago.

Giving The Finger: Known as 'gieing the finga' in Neddish. The 'go swizzle' salute when there's a squad of you having your photo taken or you appear on a *Crimewatch* caught-on-camera.

Glamour Modelling: Cash-in-hand work for short, busty women with names like Sam and Trace. 'But I don't do Continental.'

Glasgow: The City that brought us Wee Bernie, Sheena Easton and deep-fried Mars bars in batter. And Buckfast.

'But I don't do Continental...'

Gobbing/Greenies: Snot gargles evacuated in a flob. A chip adds consistency to the projectile. *See also* Flob.

Goldette: It looks like gold, it feels like gold, it smells like gold. But it's not. *See also* Bling.

Gorgeous Granny Competitions: When you get the chance to let the world know you're a great-grandma at the age of 30.

Gormless: Why Darren never gets away with it, including the DNA Test on *Trisha*.

Goths: Only found in the provinces. A chav with badly-dyed blue-black hair and a suicide complex.

Graffiti: Like hyenas marking out their territory by pissing up a tree, rat-boys use magic markers in bus shelters. They would spray paedophile if only they could spell it.

Granny Dogs: Nanna's geriatric dog called Jamelia who's blind and has a plastic cone around her head to stop her scratching her fox-mange. She grunts and farts and tries to lick her private parts. Unfortunately you eventually have Nanna put into an old people's home because she won't stop doing this.

Grebos: Hard cases (ie inflicters of Grievious Bodily Harm).

Greece: You order egg and chips and cider off the other menu, and get arrested for getting your tits out in an Orthodox church.

Gurning: A traditional face-pulling competition for pensioners with no teeth that now refers to the facial expression on pre-teen ravers who've haven't got their E to speed combination right.

Glue: Sniffed out of a carrier bag.

Gluey: One who blows in and out of said carrier bag. Even junkies sneer at him.

Gnome: Stiff little man found at the bottom of the garden. Or is that Grandad?

Goatees: Wispy effort at a moustache that makes you look more rat than man.

Graffiti gallery: Why say it, when you can spray it?

is for...

Hackett: Emblazoned on the front of your shirt. You flush little bugger, you.

Hairdresser Shop Names: Hairport, Alias Quiff & Combs, Hair Force One, Curl Up & Dye, Beauty & the Beach, Nut 'n' Nails...

Hand Gestures: Grasping your groin suggestively, swinging your hands like you're one of So Solid Crew in unison to the beat with da homeboys. But that's because Aunty Sandra can't control herself when she's snatched the linked prize at bingo.

Hanging: (1) A term for one who's a pure minger. (2) The penalty that should be suffered by pure mingers.

Misery-on-Sea.

Happy Hardcore: 'You know da score!' Whistles, glo-sticks and bucketfuls of speed. 'Big box, little box, little fish, little fish...'

Hare Coursing: It would be so much fun watching the greyhounds turn on the stupid animals that take part in this. However, it's less fun seeing them go after hares.

Harvester: Egon Ronay meets eating chips in a lay-by. Kids jump in a playpen full of plastic balls while you peruse the laminated menus.

Hash: (1) Gets Shelley off her head. (2) Corned beef – and we don't mean the flakes off Mum's corned-beef legs.

Having-A-Whitey: Too much buckaroo and Bella Brusco and you're vomin' all over your Rockports and Baybee.

Heart Attack: No longer a pitfall of old age, it's now a teenage rite of passage.

Hen Parties: Girl gangs getting shit-faced on the miniatures on a budget airline and then being done for air-rage. They always have matching hand-printed T-Shirts with logos like 'Girls on Tour 2006' or 'Buy me a lager and feel my tits'. *See also* Girl Gangs.

Hide And Heal: Go on, block out your chewies. And block out your face while you're at it. *See also* Love-bite.

Highlights: Yours make you look like a Brindle Staffordshire Bull Terrier. This is intentional.

Holiday Centres: Is this Waikiki Beach under a plastic dome? No, it's a caravan park in Pwllheli and the pensioners are pissing in the deep end of the wave pool.

Holiday Romances: You're 12, he's a Turkish waiter and you marry with your parents' blessing. Or you're a BOBFOC who gets poked rotten on an all-inclusive holiday by a beach trader half your age. Either way, you both shuffle back through customs at Gatwick with half a kilo of smack up your batty because he said he loved you. Aah! *See also* BOBFOC.

Home Video Programmes: For example: *Kirsty's Home Videos* and *You've Been Framed*. Usually involves fat fuckers falling over in paddling pools and shit-faced brides going arse-over-tit at their wedding reception – the easy way to earn some cash-in-hand.

They spell backwards...

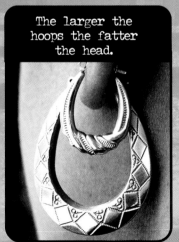

The larger the hoops the fatter the head.

Home Wine Kits: When you say your family makes wine, it's not a vineyard they own, but a shed. Funny that beetroot wine tastes like beetroot, not wine.

Hoodies: Hooded-tops worn by chavs from Stevenage who think they're Chicago gangsters. *See also* Baseball Caps.

Hooped Earrings: You're pierced, therefore you are. Big fuck-off rings gunned through every available bit of gristle. *See also* Piercings.

Horse Brasses: Hung on the brick-effect fireplace, they set off the plastic orange logs a treat.

House Names: For example: 'Versace Villa', 'Lidl's Reach', 'ASDA Heights', 'Dunroamin' and 'Dunfuckall'. Tasteful plaques to set off the satellite dish.

Humming: It's minging, it stinks, it's pure mocket, it's bogging. If you want to hide any money in your house, you stick it under the soap. Visitors wipe their feet when they leave your house.

Hyperactive Kids: A scientific way of explaining unruly brats. You say it's just something to do with the E-numbers in the pop they drink, but maybe it's something to do with the Es they're popping?

I is for...

Ibiza: Butlins on smack.

Iceland: Renowned for its tagline 'Because mums are heroes'. You can get seven frozen chickens, four bags of crinkle-cut microchips and three family-size chocolate gateaux for less than a fiver. But that's because mum's a shoplifter.

Ice Skating Shows: Basically, anything in glitter and on ice. We await news of Torvill and Dean's 20th anniversary *Bolero* come-back tour, the *John Curry Memorial Ice Spectacular* or the first performance on ice of John Inman in *Mother Goose*.

Idle: Born.

Idol: Posh.

ID Parade: The only time a ned stands next to glass without putting a brick through it.

Ignorant: What you don't know, don't hurt. It's your big fuck-off knuckle-duster that does.

In-breeding: Eleven fingers, five nipples... *See also* Incest.

Insurance jobs: A growing rural industry.

A lakeside joy-riding test centre.

innit/ɪnɪt/ *exclamation* (*BrE, slang C20th*) (1) contraction of numerous tag-questions, primarily 'Isn't it?', increasingly used to end any sentence at all; (2) expression conveying exasperation or excitement, substituted for phrases as varied as 'Do you know what I mean?' and 'Yes, I agree!'

Incest: When Dad's at home and you're bored.

Inflammable: When Mum gets too cocky lighting her farts with her Zippo and the Draylon foam-filled settee goes up like a bonfire. At least it smokes the junkies out of the estate. *See also* Zippo.

Ingot: A slab of goldette hanging off a big chunky bling necklace. *See also* Bling, Goldette.

Inhale: The involuntary lung action taken when in proximity to fags, weed, glue or Mum's butane-filled hair tongs.

Injunction: The best way to keep your ex away from his kids, well, apart from when he's in the Young Offenders' Unit.

Innit: (1) Multi-purpose word, alternative to 'D'ja nah 'ta mean?' It can be used as a threat – 'Wayne, come here, innit!'; as a question mark – 'Is it in yet, Wayne? Innit?'; or to express exasperation – 'Forget it Wayne, I'll do it myself, innit!' (2) Baybee's second name – Baybee Innit. (3) Dale Winton's *In It To Win It* during the Saturday night Thunderball draw. It involves contestants who are so thick that even *Family Fortunes* wouldn't touch them with yours.

Insurance Job: Torch your way to ready cash – set fire to the motor and the household contents. Get insurance out on the Missus and watch her go up like a burning bush. *See also* Arson.

Intoxicated: Pissed.

Intravenous Administration: The only time a ned cooks anything.

Intruder: Dad working nights.

IQ: If a sheep walked into a roomful of chavs, the IQ would double instantly.

Island Mentality: Britons never, ever, ever shall be slaves... Just pissed and stoned.

ITV: Over the years this channel has given us Joe Pasquali, Brian Conley, Bobby Davro, Ant and Dec, Hale and Pace, Cannon and Ball, *Stars in their Eyes*, *Barrymore* (before the pool episode) and *Holidays/Cruises/Neighbours/Builders* etc... *from Hell*. Leave it on full blast all day. Only change the channel for *Wife Swap*.

A rat-boy intruder working the day shift.

J is for...

Jacuzzi: Alternative to a corner bath suite. Comes in avocado, beige or burgundy and always with gold mixer taps. Something else for builders to piss into.

Jakey: An old ned. *See also* Ned.

Janners: Plymouth rat-boys. They pluralize everything and refer to the rest of the world as 'up the line'. For example: 'Egoes ligat to me, 'Oim goin' Lidls meht', reeet? An argoes, 'Oim goin' Up the loin to Car Boot.' Fockin' Mento. Innit?'

JD Sports: The Bejam of sportswear

Jaw Clenching: The facial distortion that was originally caused by hard work in cold weather, but has been set rock-solid by evolution.

JD Sports: Top spot for nicking a shell-suit.

Jewellery: Evident Goldette. *See also* Bling, Chains, Goldette.

Jewel-Encrusted Tissue Box: Classy casing for hankies. Often used by Cockney birds to blow their septums into, or Shelley when she's done too much K.

Jobseekers: Only for the allowance.

Joyriding: Kills approximately 38,000 Darrens a week and cripples a number double that who spend the rest of their lives having dinner administered through a nose tube. *See also* TWOC/twocking.

JPS: Rocket-fuelled tabs. *See also* Cigarettes, Fags.

Jumper: (1) But only Sonnetti, Ralph Lauren or Timberland worn over an un-tucked Ben Sherman shirt. (2) Garment borrowed from the cat-basket.

Junkie: A ned with a hobby. Nanna's source of income.

Jewellery: Birds wear it too
sometimes.

It's amazing what you get in crackers.

Juvenile Delinquent: A lazy ned who can't be arsed to be
a junkie.

Job Centre: Sorry? What centre?

welcome
to your

JobCentre

smash!

Joyriders: There goes
another bus shelter
full of pensioners.

K is for...

KAPPA Slappas: Girl gangs in white sports gear doing robotics outside the chip shop. They'll do anything for a chip. *See also* Girl Gangs.

Karaoke: Shit-faced hen parties singing *I Will Survive*.

Kebab: (1) Vagina. (2) Late-night scoffing frenzy during which you suck at bits of loose meat. In both cases, you always regret it in the morning.

Keeping Up With The Joneses: You don't bother doing this, you drag them down to your level and then torch the fuckers.

Ketamine: Drug also known as K. It's used to stun elephants, which given the size of the fat knackers around these days is the requisite dose. It levels off those charlie edges. When you're doing bumps of K just to get you round ASDA, you know you're in trouble.

Ketchup: On everything, including Quavers.

Kettering: Once you've been, you'll never go again.

Kevin: A chav from the 1980s, who's grown up and lives in places like Wolverhampton. He still has a perm and white terylene socks.

Kebabs: Steaming night meat for the drunk and desperate.

Ketamine: The closest thing a rat-boy gets to a chemistry GCSE.

Kick Your Head In: Bollocks to all that counselling, mediation and conflict resolution, sorting someone out with a kick in the skull never done no one no harm.

Kilroy: Orange Gob, daytime TV's not the same without you.

Kiss Me Kwik Hats: Kiss me Kwik? I wouldn't kiss you at all and especially when you've not got your teeth in.

Kit-Kat Wrappers: the old silver foil ones were great for free basing smack on a council-flat stairwell.

Knee-High Boots: Footwear of choice for BOBFOC while tripping the light fantastic and getting off with a doorman half their age. *See also* BOBFOC.

Knuckle-dusters: The reason Mum always gets first pick of the reduced-price bacon bits at the on-the-turn counter.

Krispy Kremes: The best things to eat in the world: more energizing than a charlie overdose. Deep-fried sugar-crunch doughnuts with a cream filling that provide essential manure for any facial zit-farm.

Ku Klux Klan: Who needs this jolly lot when you've got the Neighbourhood Watch?

Kwiksave: Where you go when Mum's been arrested for shoplifting in Iceland.

Ketchup... On Everything.

L is for...

Lager: Pours like a streak of piss and is drunk by a streak of piss.

Lakeside: It's like you've died and gone to shit-shop heaven...

Lambert and Butler: It's the end of the week and you can't afford Bensons.

Lambrusco: The favourite tipple of mams with prams and it also washes down the mazzies. *See also* Mazzie.

Lanzarote: Volcanic island that's prone to erupt at any minute: and that's just the shit-faced English holidaymakers.

Lakeside: Leave your fattest kid to guard your haul, while you ransack Primark.

Lapdancing Bars: Teen chavs get their tits and Caesarian scars out at designer prices.

Leopard Skin Car-Seat Covers: What Bazza uses in his Ford Astra to seduce his Shazza girlfriend; a big furry pussy covered in lots of spots. The carseat, that is.

'Leave it out!': Pronounced 'Leave it aaaht!' Cockney wanker vernacular for 'Give over!'

Lee-on-Solent: Home to pensioners and anti-asylum seeker campaigners who put the SS to shame.

Leylandi: (1) Horrible coniferous border trees used to block out the Barratt house next door. Causes neighbourly conflicts on a par with the Balkan wars. (2) Name of a glamour model.

Lidl: The shop even ram-raiders drive past.

Liebfraumilche: as if the Luftwaffe wasn't enough...

Like: The incorrect usage of. For example: 'She's like, "If you're gonna say that about me, say it to my face." And she's like, "No, you come here, the bus fare's cheaper."' Similarly, 'go' as in, 'I goes... she goes... and then I goes...'

Lakeside: Heaven.

A Lockjaw lovely.

Love-bite: You cover them up with plasters when it's your shift on the till, as it would put off the customers.

Love-rat: (1) The sort of bloke a BOBFOC meets on holiday who runs off with her life savings, after which she sells her story to *Take a Break*. (2) A rat-boy in love.

Line Dancing: Pensioners in cowboy boots doing the slosh to *Achy Breaky Heart*, followed by an achy breaky heart attack.

Litter: (1) Refuse discarded in an open or public place is one thing, but to do it in your own house is pure minging. The estate looks like a municipal dump since your kids trashed all the litter bins joy-riding; (2) rat-boys aren't born individually, they're born in litters.

Liverpool: City of culture! If the UK's a petri-dish, that is.

Loan Sharks: Like banks only they hang you upside down over the edge of a block of flats when you default.

Lobster Sunburn: When you're burnt to fuck. What's the point in going abroad unless you come back with a melanoma?

Lockjaw: Not so much a facial expression more a way of life.

is for...

Mackems and Tackems: Sunderlanders and Geordies. It's inter-town prejudice and discrimination that is completely acceptable, so they say.

Make-over: As seen in *Take a Break* or on a *Trisha* makeover special. Lip-gloss, slapped-on make-up and a dress from Hefty Hideaway are designed to transform you, but you still look like a lard-ass.

Make-up : Pancake – you slap it on, nice and thick. It's always Shrove Tuesday in Wigan.

Male Aggression Syndrome: After 16 years of being battered by your mum and force-fed E-numbers, wouldn't you rob things and set fire to them?

Malibu and Coke: Cocktail for posh cows.

Mall: Palm trees, a plastic roof, muzak, fountains, Clinton Cards and shoplifting – it's the great outdoors when you can't be arsed to watch *Trisha*. *See also* Lakeside.

Mallspeak: For example: 'Like. So. Totally. Whatever.' and, 'Talk to the hand.' *See also* Blinglish, Like.

Mams With Prams: 15 times the body mass of her boyfriend but with her own wheels.

Man Breasts: Yum, a hairy cleavage.

Manor: Cockney wanker word for the area in which you live. It is now used in Wisbech because it makes them sound hard.

Maraschino Cherries: Chuck one in a can of Breaker, to make a cocktail for the ladies.

Markets: A mixture of knock-off gear, pirate videos, boozecruize tabs and brand names that are not fake at all. *See also* Boozecruise.

> Bitch tits equals titchy bits.

Massage Parlour: The purveyors of aromatic essential oils with healing properties sensuously administered by fully-qualified Thai specialists... Or let's call it a fiver a wank.

Mams with prams: Stretch denim soldiers,
always marching, never arriving.

Down the market...

Matalan: A shop the size of an aerodrome.

Mazzie: Temazepam, a prescription drug used for recreation.

McJob: 'Do you want fries with that?'

Men and Motors: Darren's favourite TV channel. Cars before nine. Lesbian porn after. Sorted.

Mazzies: Nanna's primary source of income.

Merrydown Cider: Given the choice, even a jakey will pass this by.

Methadone: A trip to the chemist.

Minging: A compliment from one Kappa Slappa to another. *See also* Kappa Slappa.

Misogyny: Mandatory for chavs and wiggers. As in 'Bitches', 'Cocksuckers', 'Ho's' and 'Who let the dogs out?'

Mobile Discos: Available for hire at christenings, weddings, funerals, prison releases, court acquittals and ASBO liftings. Pensioners slam-dancing to the *Birdie Song*.

Mobile Phone Covers: Necessary accessory in zebra, safari, pink panther, faux-Burberry or body glitter.

Mocket: Neddish for pure humming. *See also* Humming.

Monged: Mazzies and Merrydown followed by a trip to A&E.

Mooning: Spotty and scrawny hairy doughnuts. The male equivalent of getting your tits out. Usually performed at chucking-out time, in order to pull a shag or out of the back window of the Ford Cortina that your mate's joyriding.

Moon Trackies: Astronaut shell suits. So 80s...

Morbid Obesity: It's her glands. She's got a pretty face though.

Morecambe: Apart from karaoke and street fights on the sea front, Morecambe also boasts one of the highest incidences of drug dependency in the UK; and that's just the pensioners. It's a pity the Mr Blobby theme park in pink and yellow polka dots was abandoned. Talk about a seaside 'trip'.

Mother and Daughter 'Sisters': You and your daughter say you're each other's best mates – you look and dress the same and go out clubbing together to trap off. You sing *Sisters* on a karaoke challenge, while the lads watching toss a coin to decide which one gets the old, raddled one. We await evidence of a daughter, mum and gran going out as a threesome, getting shit-faced and competing to be the first one to cop off.

Bad hair... ...even worse.

From mother to daughter: Hair of the dog, anyone?

Motorway Service Stations: The stop-off for chips and a piss-up for people in big coaches and camper vans. You yak it up all up on the hard shoulder afterwards.

Mottled Blue Thighs: Milk bottle legs that have curdled into Stilton.

Mobile phone covers: You're never too young to accessorize...

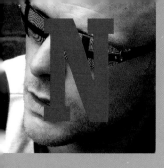

N is for...

Nail Bars: Pink-painted talons with goldette hoop insertions. Like, so nasty.

Name and Shame Campaigns: Local celebrity. You've got an ASBO and you're in the papers.

Names: Chardonnay, Stellar, Bacardi, Aftershoque, Britney, Beyoncé, Whitney, Orlando, Paris, Brooklyn, Aya Napa, Barry, Wayne, Craig, Craigette, Donatella, Daryl, Dave, Tony, Sharon, Stacey, Kylie, Innit.

Nanna: (1) Just like Mum but with foamy legs and no teeth. She sells her prescriptions on to the rat-boy junkies on the estate. (2) Woman who runs off with Mum's new boyfriend and they all have a scrap on a *Trisha* reunion.

Nationalism: England's the best country in the world because, well, you come from it. From flags to face paint, bunting to bed covers, the new religion of English nationalism and the yobcrucifix of St. George have overtaken the nation. Well what else do we sorry fuckers have to cheer about? Follow your spirit and, upon this charge 'Cry God for Harry, England and St. George'. Innit.

Nail shops: Essential hardware

Nanna: She's well 'ard!

St. George at ASDA.

It started with a cross...

Nature versus nurture: Either way, neuter.

Nazism: Too liberal a political affiliation. Darth Vadar is a good stab at where you sit on the political spectrum.

Neanderthal: Who said these boys were extinct? Haven't you been to Wisbech Horsefair?

Necklace: Always in goldette from Elizabeth Duke or the shopping channel. The girls who wear these will never have a pearl necklace; they'll swallow if you give them a chip.

Ned: A chav from Scotland. 'Och aye, innit. Cunt'.

Needles: Shelley's knitting. Darren's injecting. They swap needles at half-time, so he can fend off his hallucinations and she can freebase to *Coronation Street*.

Negative: Double: 'I never done nothing'. Triple: 'I ain't never done nothing.' Quadruple: 'I ain't never done nothing, so I ain't.'

Neighbourliness: Robbing next-door when they've gone out, so as not to disturb them.

Neighbours From Hell: One sure way of getting on the TV, when even *Ibiza/Ayia Napa/Southend Uncovered* or *How Clean Is Your House?* won't touch you.

Nerves: Spurious, non-specific illness, which is a sure-fire winner to award you top whack disability living allowance, while you've a nice little sideline plastering or robbing old grannies' houses. 'It's my nerves, Doctor said.'

Net Curtains: Frilly and gathered in the middle so that they look like the backside of a woman who's got her knickers caught up in her dress after visiting the ladies.

Nicking: Robbing.

Nicotine: Colour of your walls, teeth and Baybee.

Nickelson: Where you learnt to read Part II.

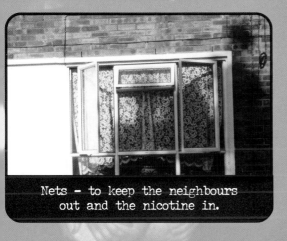
Nets - to keep the neighbours
out and the nicotine in.

Nike: Make of Aunty Sandra's wedding dress the third time around.

Non-entity: If you had any ambition or a personality, you'd have gone a long way. But you haven't. The Park and Ride is as far as you'll go.

Nouveaux Riche: Like Posh, you're rich as fook, but still common as mook. Remote control garage doors, holiday homes in Malaga, ten soft tops in the drive, chiming gates and a big fuck-off static in Pwllheli. You've probably won the Lottery or robbed a bank. That, or you'll have a criminal record under your belt; just like Posh.

Nutrition: Sunny D with your bags of chips.

Nympho: Kerb-crawling on her disabled scooter at Aunty Trish's age is like, so gross.

Nouveau Shite...

O is for...

Oaf: An awkward lout or stupid person. Well, that's narrowed the field...

Obesity: *See* Morbid Obesity Syndrome.

Obscene: Pirate snuff movies from the market or anything that comes out of a Kappa Slappa's mouth. *See also* X-rated.

Odour: Your house is humming. No wonder the mice wear overalls. *See also* Humming, Mocket.

Offensive Hairstyles: Hair do's? Hair don'ts! Home perms and bleaching kits; Mum's fuzz-ball helmet after her 'forest murmurs and conker' rinse or rat-boys with Beckham mohawks. Call the hair police! *See also* Gelled Fringe, Perm, Shit For Hair.

Off-Licence: Also known as the offie. The beacons by which junkies navigate themselves away from bus shelters.

Oi: As in 'Oi, what you fuckin' lookin at?' or 'Oi, you sitting on my fags?'

Old Slag: You open your legs more than your pension book and your skirts are so short that when you cross your legs on the bar stool the whole pub sees your stretch marks. Don't forget to drop your teeth in the glass before switching off the light.

One-Armed Bandit: A fruit machine. Mum needs two stools to play the one-armed bandit while she's concentrating on her next nudge in the interval at bingo. That's one stool per bum cheek.

One Hell Of A Rotten Face: BOBFOC, say-no-more. *See* BOBFOC.

On-The-Turn Counter: Yesterday's bread and rancid cream cakes reduced to clear.

Oozing Skin Condition: No matter how much blusher and foundation you wear, skin will always out. Your cheeks are so close to rhino skin that you can strike a match off them to light your crack.

Orange Gob: BOBFOCs or blokes that look like Kilroy.

Orange Sunbed Tan: *See* Tanning Salons.

Ornaments: Cheap and horrible, just like Aunty Trish. *See* Collectibles, Royal Memorabilia.

Outside: As in, 'Let's sort this outside.'

Overdressed: You look like a dog's dinner as you clatter down to Lidl in full fur coat and stilettos.

Ornaments: Where better to stash your gear?

Bandits: One-armed not bum, that is.

is for...

Pebble Dashing: Makes your satellite dish feel less ugly

Page Three: 'Show us your charms!'; 'Show us your Page Threes'. Like footballers' wives, Page Three girls only come from Cheshire or Essex and don't do continental. *See also* Footballers' Wives, Glamour Modelling.

Pampers: A wedding present.

Patio: Gardens for the upwardly mobile, as in 'Fancy a G&T on the patio, Trace?'. You buy one on tick but – like a form of human bondage – were too thick to realize 120 months was in fact 10 years.

Pebble Dashing: (1) Disgusting render for the front of your house. (2) What you do after a session at an All-You-Can-Eat restaurant and 12 pints. (3) What Baybee does when it swallows that E you hid under the settee.

IMN ARSOL 1

People's Princess: She's the candle in the wind, England's Rose, Saint Di etc. She's also available in a series of tasteful figurines available from Franklin Mint. Stick her on top of the flat-screen.

Perm: (1) The result of a home-perm kit, slapped down with a litre of hair gel. (2) Mum's fuzz-ball perm, set so hard that it withstands the hurricane on the all-inclusive in the Dominican Republic. *See also* Offensive hairstyles.

Peroxide: Get your roots done or go for a Myra Hindley.

Personalized Registration Plate: Unfortunately you're too piss poor to afford WANKER1 out of *Exchange & Mart*, otherwise you'd be ram-raiding Poundstretcher with it.

Pet Beauty: Dogs with perms – taking their animals for a blow dry at the beautician.

Peterborough: 1960s new town with probably the fattest, least-educated people in the country, but they are fucking hard. Consequently there are high levels of demand for cross-breeding with people from elsewhere.

Pet Funeral: You still mourn Jamelia, the family's American Pit Bull that mauled your own grandson and which they made you put down under the Dangerous Dogs Act. *See also* Dangerous Dogs.

Gelled perm? Forest fire.

Pet Rescue: Serious drama.

Piece: (1) Gun. (2) Of piss: i.e. you.

Piercings: On eyebrows, belly buttons, genitals and, of course, Baybee and followed by septic discharge. *See also* Earrings, Eyebrow Piercing.

Pigeon-Racing: Your forefathers used to breed these rats with wings that shit all over the estate but you're too off your face to continue the tradition. The only time you'll handle a pigeon these days is to sew smack into its gizzards and bung it over the prison wall to one of your mates.

Fucking hard.

67

Pizza parlours: It's 5am and
Kentucky's shut...

P

Plastering: A skill required by either builders or beauty therapists: 'Get the trowel out, love, nice and thick.' *See also* Beauty Therapy.

Plastic Surgery: Package deal for £200 all-in that's performed by unlicensed cowboy surgeons who moved with the market when the bottom fell out of back-street abortions in the late 1960s. They throw in a face lift and liposuction followed by an interview with ITV's *Plastic Surgery from Hell*.

Plastic Tits: A thirteenth birthday present for Chardonnay. They're filled with so much silicone that they explode in midair en route to the all-inclusive.

Pikey: Term of abuse for those deemed lower down the social scale. And there's always someone lower.

Pirate: Knock-off videos and DVDs. *Death Wish XVII* isn't so good when it's been filmed from the back of a Bankok picture house with Thai subtitles, and you can hear the sound of ping pong balls and ladyboys scoffing popcorn.

Piss Elegant: Posh stuff at affordable prices. *See also* Capo Di Monte, Gay Hotels.

Pizza Face: How eating too much junk puts zombie-latex to shame. Symptoms include yellowheads, blackheads, red zits, flaking eczema, in-growing hairs, septic cold sores, scurvy, trench foot and fox-mange.

Pizza Parlour: The restaurant where you eat continental-style. Get healthy with a bowlful of potato salad covered with those crispy bacon bits, from the £5 all-you-care-to-eat buffet.

Poem: As in obituaries in local newspapers. For example:

'"Look here," St Peter said,
"The best is yet to come."
He opened wide the Pearly Gates,
And in walked Mum.'

or

'The angels took Darren from us,
He nicked a car then gone,
Joyriding, he hit a bus-shelter,
And died aged twenty-one.'

See also Funeral.

Police: (1) Police car chases caught on CCTV offering distance learning for joyriders. (2) *The Bill*.

Police Van: The late-night alternative to a taxi.

68

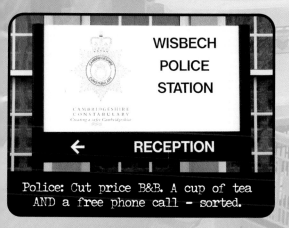

Police: Cut price B&B. A cup of tea AND a free phone call - sorted.

Post-pub grub: Dog burger anyone?

Politics: This means absolutely nothing to you, although you might vote BNP or for Orange Gob if he ever stands again.

Posh: (1) You get out of the bath for a piss. (2) A streak of piss.

Posse: Nanna's mates.

Post-Pub Grub: Vindaloo, lager and vomiting it all up on the pavement outside Argos. Cut out the middle-man and flush it straight down the bog.

The ever-faithful poundshop.

'How much is this?' 'Pahnd'. 'And this?' 'Pahnd'. 'And this?' 'F*** off.'

A jar in the pub that time forgot.

A dead pub usually gets cremated.

Pot Pourri: Sweepings from a forest floor drenched in perfume not dissimilar to cat's pee. Stick it on the cistern, next to the toilet roll dolly, to detract from the stench of the piss stains on the carpet.

Poundshops: When even Lidl is too posh.

Prison: Your drugs visit you each week in your girlfriend's snatch.

Pram: Mode of transport for morbidly-obese kids pre-joyriding.

Pram Face: Found from Croydon to Glasgow.

Precinct: Junkies jacking-up under the escalators and the place where Grandad took his final tumble. *See also* Mall.

Price Tag: Guidelines for how much your fence pays you to handle the shit you've shoplifted.

Prison: The place to go when no one else will have you because you can't stop setting fire to things. You get SKY Sports all day, but you have to watch your Gary.

Professional Family Photographs: Oil-on-canvas effect 'portraits' so fuzzed out with gauze that all that's visible in the mist is Nanna's baseball cap and the pet pit bull.

Pubs: 1950s carpeting and chain-smoking pensioners. Place to buy knock-off goods from tattooed junkies.

Q is for...

Qualifications: There are only two qualifications: beauty therapy or leisure studies. Either way, you'll end up with a McJob, in prison or on the dole.

Quality Street: Quality is the chocolate nut in the purple cellophane. It certainly isn't the road you live on.

Quarter Pounder: Rissoles consisting of ear-holes, eye-holes and arse-holes. And 'cheese'.

Quavers: Breakfast cereal.

Queer Bashing: But Dale Winton's OK.

Questions Not Statements: Also known as high rise terminals; this is speech in which every sentence ends with an interrogative tone so that it sounds like a question. It all started with *Neighbours* and *Home and Away*. For example: 'My name's Chardonnay, OK?', 'I come from Plymouth?', 'Why are you arresting me?', 'I just thrown a bockle at someone and I'm not never going into that police van, so I ain't?' and 'This is like, so totally? Standard? Aye?!?'

Queue: Thing that asylum seekers are always jumping, or that's what you say when you're throwing petrol bombs at their bed and breakfast.

Quiche: Cheesy egg with broccoli bits for posh people. Flan to the rest of us.

Quickie: On the back seat of Darren's Vauxhall Nova.

Quiz Shows: Pig-shit thickos competing for caravans and garden furniture by spinning a wheel. Bring back Bullseye.

Quavers for breakfast.

R is for...

Racism: It's what do-gooders go on about. You're not a racist, right, but you just can't stand those asylum seekers. You think black people are cool, innit, but fail to see the connection between attacking those seeking political asylum and other forms of xenophobia.

Radio One: Always on full-blast, even during Grandad's wake.

Radio Wisbech: Great for *Pram-Swap Challenge* and *Desert Island Turnips*.

Ram-raiding: Out-of-hours drive-thru' shopping.

Rap/R&B: Alternative to chart. *See also* Chart.

Rat-boys: They never grow higher than five feet tall, their fingers stink of fags and they sire the offspring of lasses 15 times their own body mass. There are many varieties: the common rat-boy; the lesser-zitted variety; the faux-Burberry crested; and the great ginger-minger. All can be found thieving in baseball caps, ram-raiding, car-jacking, having DNA tests on *Trisha* and joyriding themselves into a wheelchair after turning over that last Ford Capri. But at least they made it onto *Police, Camera, Action!*

Ratting: Ripping rats (not rat-boys) apart for fun as enjoyed by salt-of-the-earth working-class huntsmen. Sometimes they let their terriers have a go too.

Readers' Wives: Full tit and minge beautifully photographed next to the chip-pan. Now the world is Mum's gynaeocologist, not just Uncle Dave.

Reality TV: Jade. QED.

Red Sauce: On everything, even Quavers.

Rent: (1) A payment for accommodation. (2) A male prostitute. Either way, it's good money wasted on a dirty old hole.

Replacement Windows: An expensive way of devaluing your property. The lattice or criss-cross style will set off the Capo Di Monte a treat.

Restraining Order: The reason why Darren's never around Baybee.

Ringtones: The theme from *Titanic* or anything by Peter Andre in poly- and mono-tones.

Rizlas: Used for bombing speed when it's too sticky to snort.

Robbing: Rat-boy pastime. If you hadn't borrowed Nanna's tights to put over your head, you wouldn't be gagging over the till.

Rochester: Like Dagenham, just more so.

Rough as Fuck: *See* BOBFOC.

Royal Memorabilia: They say you shouldn't attack the Royal Family because they can't answer back, and that's especially true when they're dead, so why not dance on their graves and commemorate their coming off the taxpayers' expense with hideous memorabilia? The limited-edition *Candle in the Wind* clock looks great on top of the flat-screen. We await production of a souvenir dog bowl commemorating the death of the Queen's favourite pet Corgi to go alongside the Princess Margaret limited-edition ornamental intravenous drip in porcelain.

Rozzers: The Filth, The Fuzz, The Pigs, The Scum, The Old Bill, the bloke who stuffs you in the back of a van so often they've given you a personalised holding cell.

Rudeboys: Albino Jamaicans, living in Guildford. Identified by their mode of speech, for example: 'Razklat. Standard, innit... Aye!'

Common Ratboy, *rattus vulgaris*

'God Save the Queen...'

S is for...

Samsara: An incredibly strong perfume that obscures fags, booze and the stench of vomit.

Satellite Dish: All that extra-terrestrial technology and scientific innovation just so that you can see re-runs of *Jerry Springer*, *Trisha* and *Kilroy*.

Scallies: Rat-boys living near Mersey tunnel singing *Danny Boy*.

School: Place where Mum comes to shout the odds, and knocks seven bells out of the teachers if they so much as give you a funny look. She then has a blast from the glue sniffers' carrier bags on her way out of the gates.

Scratchcards: If you spend £500 a week on these, you're quids in when you win £10 and a Poundstretcher trolley-grab.

Sengers: Kappa-Slappas from the rougher parts of Scotland.

Settee: This is where you'll find Nanna when she's not dealing. It's the big, knackered and bust-up old thing that's found slumped in front of the TV. The settee, however, is still in pristine condition.

Satellite dishes: Which way is Sky Sports?

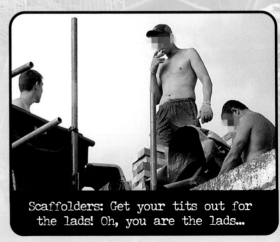

Scaffolders: Get your tits out for the lads! Oh, you are the lads...

Shagpile: A long-haired carpet that's ideal for retaining the dog shit brought in on shoes and impossible to clean.

Shell Suits: They're easy care, wash-'n'-go and look nice with trainers. Grandad's buried in his.

Shit For Hair: For example: the Beckham mohawk, fat slag short cuts, gelled fringes and top-knot scrunchies in a pineapple. *See also* Offensive Hairstyles.

Shit Shops: End of Clearance bargain basements where nothing's worth nicking.

Shoplifting: Career.

Shopping Channel: Where you can buy porcelain doll collections and goldette jewellery. All lovingly made by 6-year-old Filipinos.

Shopping Trolley: (1) A portable crèche at Poundstretcher. (2) An object that rat-boys throw in a canal.

Shaz: Bazza's girlie. Identified by her peroxide perm and the fact that she teeters around in stilettos without a coat whatever the weather. *See also* Bazza.

Sickies: Everyone's allowed six months of statutory sick leave a year, but then you get caught on camera nicking tiles off a roof while you're off for a bad back, or your nerves.

Sink Estates: The whole estate's on an ASBO. Even the grannies are joyriding.

Skip: A vestibule for dumping your shit in.

Shit for hair...

Shagpile: Amazing what you can do with those offcuts

Skip-cap: A vestibule for shit-heads and smack-heads.

Sky: Great sport.

Smack: (1) A battering you give your kids. (2) A battering you give your veins. Either way, it's enjoyment when there's fuck all else to do.

Smoking: Having a fag. Not to be confused with queer bashing. *See also* Cigarettes, Tabs.

Getting off your trolley if you're not a junkie.

No Smoking? What do you f*cking mean?

Smoking In The Street: It proves you're multi-skilled, even if you can't get a proper drag on it.

Smoking While Pregnant: Surest way of breeding something small and ugly.

Snooker: A vision of hell with waistcoats in it. Fact: all snooker players come from Romford.

Social Club: Where BOBFOCs do their step-aerobics and get bollocksed on Barley Wine chasers of a Saturday night.

Social Security: A supplementary state income to thieving.

Social Worker: A state-sponsored friend who tells you not to wash-up in the water you've been soaking Baybee's shitty nappies in.

Southend: Cockney wankers by the sea singing *Vindaloo*.

Sovereign Rings: more commonly known as sovvy rings. You asked for one of these because they're smart, they make you look really hard and they maim in a fight. A range for men is available too.

Spearmint Rhino: You want that young one from Uzbekistan to get back on her pole because it's like a mouse's ear.

Speccy: Spectrum Cider.

Special Moment: Two pints of lager.

Speed: The only reason you get about of bed before noon, unless it's giro day or a *Trisha* reunion.

Spirituality: The things that you believe in: alien abduction; that the reception for your satellite dish hasn't been the same since Grandad passed away and that Diana's being looked after by Mother Teresa in Heaven. One day you'll do a pilgrimage to Graceland.

Squad: Collective noun for rat-boys.

Steroids: You're so pumped up that your brain's frazzled and you've serious psychiatric problems, from aggressive behavior to delusions and profound paranoia... And you look like Chris Quentin.

Sovvys: There just aren't enough fingers on one hand.

Stilettos: High-rise mams with prams or a pair of slippers for Shaz.

Streak Of Piss: You'll know one when you see one, as he's usually running down the street with your alloys.

Supersize: Everything, but especially your burger and fries.

Super Strength Lager: There's nothing like cracking open a big tinnie to start the day. But then Mum could never be arsed with breakfast.

Spirituality. Elvis is out there, with Shergar and Diana.

Shaz's stillies: Certain death for the ceiling of your Escort convertible.

T is for...

Tagging Device: It chafes your ankle, but you still get to rob things.

Take a Break: In our view, a wank-mag for any true connoisseur of peasant culture. Highlights include Brainwaves Roadshow (top tips like 'stencil your toilet seat and turn it into a garden ornament'), Heartbeats, Beauty Lab, Boot Sale Tales, My Operation, a five-minute supermarket grab, competitions, crosswords and more magic makeovers than you can shake a stick at. Readers' Reality has the sort of real-life stories that even *Trisha* would reject for being implausible. This magazine is tops!

Tanning Salons: How to become a raddled tanorexic the fast way.

Lobster tanning on the beach...

Tattoos: Celtic bands imprinted on flabby old bingo wings or Britney Spears-style fairies and flags of St. George tattooed on hairy arses. *See also* Art.

Tea: Tea is dinner, dinner is lunch and breakfast is Quavers.

Teenage Dads: High sperm counts and low IQs. As seen on *Trisha*.

Teeth: They've all fallen out due to speed abuse, been sold to buy smack or both. You've got your wallies in your zip-up bum bag so you don't swallow them when you're gurning at the rave. *See also* Dentistry, False Teeth.

Telly: (1) Item carried down the street, especially after a ram-raid or a riot. (2) The only time you'll be on it is coming out of the back of a van with a blanket over your head. *See also* Flat-screen TV.

Tenerife: Budget airline long-haul destination. Pensioners sunning themselves on the arse-end of a volcano.

10-Minute Free-View: Spanking the monkey Travelodge-style. Hard-core German porn set to elevator muzak, only free. Mind you don't get it all over the polyester bedspread.

Tennent's Super: The top tinnie drink. To be savoured while sat on a park bench shouting obscenities at passers-by or from the inside of a skip. *See also* Tinnies.

Testosterone: The hormone that leads to swagger-

The tit thong in all its glory.

ing around, battering anyone nearby and ending up in the back of a police van. And that's just the birds.

Texting: The written word. Text abbreviations are used for everything. For example: Name: R@boy, Previous Jobs: U wht? Hobbies: procre8ing, wtchng *Trisha* etc.

What, no Carnation cream?

Theme Parks: Donuts, water splashes, chips in mayonnaise and the chance to vomit on the coach going home.

Theme Pubs: Plastic plants and lager that tastes of piss.

Thick Shakes: If every mam with pram sucked into her thick shake simultaneously the windows at Lakeside would cave in. Available in brown, pink and yellow flavours.

Thunderball Rollover: Do them all and win piss all. But you get to watch Dale Winton's *In It To Win It*.

Time Shares: Two weeks all-inclusive on a building site on the Algarve... But you get the weather.

Tinned Fruit: Bits of swede and turnip in sugared water. You get a round of applause if you find a red glacé cherry.

Tinnies: Lager, Lager, Lager! Or Fruit.

Tit Thong: As pioneered by TV's Beverley Callard. Part breast strap, part mammary G-String or just an ingenious way to camouflage 40+ crepe cleavage with extra bling?

Theme Parks: A wonder world of queuing in the pissing rain.

Tracksuits: Going nowhere, only faster.

dents back to the Blackbird Leys with a blade held to their neck.

Tracksuit: Elasticated bum-bags with go-faster stripes that are also known as trackies. *See also* Shell Suits.

Trainers: They're always pristine and immaculate with laces that are threaded like a work of art. You wear white ones in winter so that the rozzers can't see your footprints in the snow. Footwear of status (except for the tagging device).

Trisha: Morning TV show featuring morbidly obese people with no teeth having DNA tests for popular entertainment. They go back on the show after the counselling so that the audience can laugh at them again. The best thing to come out of Norwich since the A47. But that takes you to Wisbech.

Tits: You're either getting them out or enlarging them. *See also* Plastic Tits.

Trolley Dollies: Camp skivvies in the skies, smothered in fake tan. Chicken or fish? They love chicken but they hate fish.

Toilet Roll Doll: A plastic doll with an embroidered dress that sits on the cistern and has a bog-roll up her snatch.

Trompe L'Oeil: Tacky murals that create illusions of space through perspective. French for 'trick of the eye'. And when you see one of these murals you know they're playing a right fucking joke on you. It's Vimuraland on acid. All that's missing is Hilda Ogden's three ducks. Just nasty.

Tongue Piercing: You were inarticulate, now you're incomprehensible. Second operation on Baybee after she's had her ears gunned. *See also* Piercings.

Totally: Pronounced in a faux-American accent: e.g. 'It's like so, towdally bad.'

Truant Officer: The wagger woman.

Townies: Term originating in Oxford. Girl-gangs getting their tits out among the dreaming spires, and chavs joyriding stu-

TWOC/Twocking: Taking Without Owner's Consent. Also known as joyriding.

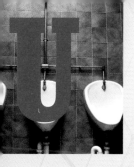

U is for...

Ubiquitous: Every town looks the same nowadays. Like dog shit, the rat-boys are everywhere.

UK Gold: All those episodes of *The Bill*, plus re-runs of *Kilroy*.

Unconscious: The state of Shelley after she's been on the mazzies and Merrydown. It's also the state of Aunty Sandra after she's drunk a bucket after winning the big prize at the bingo. *See also* A&E.

Uncouth: If you can't express yourself in more eloquent terms, best keep your gob shut, eh?

Under-arm Cellulite: *See* Bingo Wings.

Uneducated: What do you mean, you're uneducated? Prison taught you everything you need to know. That, and *Trisha*.

Ungrammatical: 'It's like so not on man, I ain't never done nothing so I ain't, innit?' *See also* Negative.

Uninsurable: A Boyracer's alloyed car the seventh time he's wrapped it around a chevron. Well, that's if it's his car in the first place.

Units: Fitted. A setting under strip lighting for the crystal decanter you were given in exchange for the coupons from all those packets of fags you smoked.

Like a pharmacy, but stinks of piss.

Universal Language: Innit! Innit?

Unwomanly Behaviour: Aunty Trish getting her kebab out for passing buses.

Urinal: Dealing area. Used to be full of respectable homosexuals doing things with glory holes.

UV Lights in Public Toilets: So junkies can't see their veins to jam stuff into them, you can't shoot-up, but you can snort your K and pretend you're in a nightclub. Best example formerly located at Wigan North Western train station.

V is for...

Valentine: Love is breaking the court injunction you had taken out on your ex and then calling the police when you start knocking seven bells out of each other because you're shit-faced on Diamond White. But at least you sent each other fuck-off big Valentine's Day cards.

Valium: When even Ecstasy won't level you off.

Vanilla: 'I said no Gary, Gary! Just vanilla, innit!'

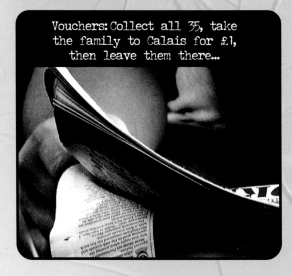

Vouchers: Collect all 35, take the family to Calais for £1, then leave them there...

Varnish: The substance that mams with prams sniff in a nail bar.

Vast Arse: It resembles the back end of a bus and is only ever found in leggings.

Vauxhall Novas: The conveyance of choice for the Jedi Knights of Wisbech. May the Force be with you... The power certainly isn't.

Veins: Neds said goodbye to theirs years ago.

Velour: The material of the zip-up shell suit that Mum uses for knocking about in. Not the one she uses for court appearances.

Verbal Dyslexia: For example: 'skellington' for skeleton; 'Alstation' for Alsatian and 'bockle' for bottle.

Versace: Saddam Hussein art meets Draylon. A pair of Versace slacks will set you back about £40k. We have a sighting of a Versace wall-mounted towel rail in Billericay.

Very Short Skirt: The world's a BOBFOC's gynaecologist.

Vest: Preferably string and worn with tattoos and a gammy pair o' old terylene jogging pants.

Viagra: A BOBFOC never leaves without a handful of these and a bag for her head in her clutch bag. *See* BOBFOC.

Vigilantes: Socially-aware mams with prams egged on by name-and-shame campaigns in the tabloid press.

Vomit: Kentucky re-wind! Everybody say, 'Bo!' Don't vomit on your own doorstep – leave it to the smack-heads in your stairwell.

Vouchers: Retired White Trash spend the whole week cutting out vouchers from free newspapers promising 5p off a packet of Craven As.

VPL: The visible panty line. In fact, your whole arse is visible and hanging out.

V-sign: Giving the finger when you want to look posh.

Vulgar: What's wrong with a jewel-encrusted tissue box?

Vandalism: Always gets a laugh.

Vomit: Fast food in reverse.

W is for...

Wagon Wheel: (1) An item propped next to the rockery and the satellite dish that shows you've bought your council house. (2) Slimmers' chocolate for the morbidly obese.

Wales: Nation that pisses in the Brummies water supply.

Walloping: You do it around the kid's head with a bottle of Sunny D, across the legs or straight in the gob in the middle of Lidl. Such violent abuse in public is completely in order and completely different to what paedophiles do.

Water Features: (1) Cascading and ornamental. (2) Football fans with big tinnies pissing all over your front garden.

Weapon: Either a gun or a cock. Pity your cock's not firing blanks.

Webcam: Aunty Trish's source of extra pin-money. She does something with a penny whistle as a gimmick.

Weddings: First weddings are in a church, second weddings are in the registry office and third and further weddings are on a beach in the tropics. We pay tribute to the bride on ITV's

Water features:
Classy, like.

Weddings from Hell who was arrested at her own wedding reception and thrown into the back of a police van. That's after she had whacked her mum in the face and called her husband a cunt. *See also* Beach Wedding, Church.

Weed: Junky rat-boys going organic.

Welt: The unhealed abscess left after a love-bite, fag burn, zit or ripped-out piercing.

Wet-Look Gel: Spray it, mousse it and then gel it to fuck. *See also* Gelled Fringe, Offensive Hairstyles.

Whale Tails: Those cheap plastic bits boyracers stick on the back of their cars. Not to be confused with the humpback, killer and sperm varieties. That's the boyracers who drive them.

Whatever: As in 'It's like, so... whatever!' Thumbs together now to show the W-sign.

What the Sun Says: 'Kill an Argie, Win a Metro'; 'Send them back'; 'Phew Wotta Scorcher!'; 'Get Your Tits Out!' It's common sense.

White Van Man: (1) The conscience of the nation in cement, paint, food or piss-splattered sportswear. (2) The bloke who drives Mum off when her careworker sections her.

Wife Beater: (1) Men Behaving Badly. (N.B. NOT to be confused with Lee Chapman, husband of *Men Behaving Badly*'s Leslie Ash. (2) A brand of lager. (3) A Cocktail: mix Special Brew beer and White Lightning cider with a shot of Jack Daniels, tequila and vodka in a pint glass. Then fill a shot glass with Baileys and drop into said pint glass. And then stick the toilet-roll in the fridge overnight.

Wiggers: You want to be black but you're too uncool. And you're also white.

Wiggerspeak: The speech of wiggers, for example: 'Yo bitch, slip

Wife-beater: Cocktail for men.

White van man's piss stains.

White van man to the rescue.

Wisbech: Capital of the Fens.

me dem skinz, mo'va fucka!' – Darren from Wisbech asking his gran for one of her fags.

Wisbech: Town situated 25 miles northwest of Peterborough with a population of 19,000 linked via the A47 to King's Lynn. Here, Tony Martin is God.

Wrestling: Saturdays are cack without the likes of Catweasel, Big Daddy, Giant Haystacks and Mick McManus belting the shit out of each other on telly. The American stuff's for poofs.

Wrexham: A real welcome in the Welsh Hillside. 'You are entering an area controlled by CCTV.' Home of anti-social behaviour, arson, and the 'Wild West' Caia Park Estate...

Wrestling: sport of kings.

X is for...

X: Your signature for Job Seekers' Allowance, but that's because the closest you got to school was glue-sniffing at the gates.

Xenophobia: You hate everyone, especially that lot in the next street.

Xmas Club: Saving scheme that enables its members to spend the equivalent of Belorussia's GDP on Xmas presents each year. Why is it that someone called Aunty Pat always runs off with the Xmas club money?

Xmas Decorations: You might live in a pebble-dashed council

Xmas in Hell...

house at the arse-end of an estate but come Xmas it lights up like the bombing of Fallujah. Decorations go up in August and come down in the following July.

XR3: Always with full body kit.

X-rated: Pirate video nasties or snuff cannibal movies, such as *Vampire Baby Executions* and *Zombie Kebab Eaters From Uranus* watched as family entertainment. *See also* Pirate.

Y is for...

Yam-Yams: Completely incomprehensible brummies, which is just as well really because they all talk a load of pointless shit. For example: 'Ow yow gooin, mert?', 'R, oim bostin' aye oi?', 'Bostin' am ya?', 'R oim avin' a Balti down the Bull Ring', 'Bostin', etc. etc.

Yard Of Ale: Aunty Sandra finds glugging down two-and-a-half pints of lager a piece of piss on her bingo night. It's the drinking back up of the sick she's projectile vomited into the glass that's the difficult part.

Da yoof of today.

Yarnley: Staffordshire village where it seems half the under 16 population was put on an ASBO. The other half are already in a Young Offenders Unit.

Yellow: (1) The colour of fingers, teeth or fringes. (2) The colour of the piss-filled bockle – weapon of choice come closing time. (3) The soles of your feet before the smoking-related amputation.

An organic petrol bomb...

Yob Culture: Disgusting anti-social behaviour that involves drinking, smashing bottles and nicking car stereos. But then Mum's had a lot of time on her hands since the bingo took out an injunction against her.

Yo' Man: Oh no, Mum's seen you in the bus shelter with your chav mates and she wants to neck your GHB.

Young Offender's Units: Finishing schools/career training.

Youth: Of today. Parents with tagging devices freebasing smack The future belongs to you.

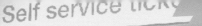
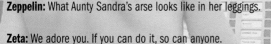

Zeppelin: What Aunty Sandra's arse looks like in her leggings.

Zeta: We adore you. If you can do it, so can anyone.

Zimmer Frames: (1) A walking support for morbidly obese pre-teens or joyriding 13 year olds who've collided with a bus shelter full of pensioners. (2) The device Nanna hides her smack in when she's dealing outside Iceland.

Zippo: What you use to light your weed, or start a claim on the insurance.

Zits: Facial bubble wrap that can be popped anywhere as there will always be more where they came from. They look like weeping fried eggs mixed with pizza.

Zodiac: (1) Mystic Meg's lottery numbers. (2) Dena's Life Stars in *Take a Break*. (3) Hard drink guzzled by jakeys.

Zombies: The living dead. But then again, a life in Wisbech is the living death.

Zoo: Place where you should be kept.

ZZZZZZ: Is this the result of too many Mazzies and Merrydown in front of daytime TV or is it the end?

'Can I dip a chip in your zit?'

Zzz...

Photography credits:

All photographs taken by Jamie Same, apart from:

pp 89 bottom left (Adam Morris).

Cover: front, back & spine (background); pp 1; 2; 3; 6—7 (map); 10 top; 12 bottom; 16 bottom; 18 bottom right; 26 top; top, middle & bottom left; 30 bottom left; 33 top left, middle, bottom right; 35 bottom; 36; 38 top; 39; 46; 47 top & centre right; 48 bottom right; 50 top left; 53 bottom; 55 bottom right; 66 centre, bottom; 68 bottom; 76; 84 top left; 85 bottom left; 89 top right; 91 top left; 92 bottom right (Alan Marshall).

pp 5 right; 35 centre right; 63; 69 top right; 70 bottom left (Gareth Jones).

pp 87 top right (Hannah Blake).

pp 85 bottom left (Jon Gilbody).

pp 65 bottom right (Lee Quick).

All background images by Alan Marshall, apart from:

pp 8—11; 60—63; 94—95 (Gareth Jones).

pp 64—65; 90—91 (Jamie Same).

pp 42—45 (John Baxter).

Thanks also go out to Ronan and Ciaran for giving it the big finger, and to Caff for the wicked motor on page 1.

God bless...

Lee Quick, Darren Pike and Jamie Same
dedicate this book to their families and friends
for the inspiration...

THE END